SMILE

SMILE

Alfred Gremsly

Printed in the United States of America.

Published by Poetic Justice Books
Port Saint Lucie, Florida
www.poeticjusticebooks.com

ISBN: 978-1-950433-02-5

FIRST EDITION
10 9 8 7 6 5 4 3 2 1

National Suicide Prevention Lifeline
1-800-273-8255
suicidepreventionlifeline.org

This is a story of pain and hurt
This is a story I barely survived
This is the book I had to write
This is the book that kept me alive

This book is a poem to myself

table of contents

SMILE

Chapter 1

Love Me
Like You
Hate Me

Umbilical

In the womb
I could not see
uncertain fates
surrounding me
nor yet knowing
birth would be
the feeding tube
for misery

The Game of Life

Roulette
is getting
out of bed
everyday
and facing
a world
we're forced
to play
with a
shaky finger
and a
nervous aim
we're born
in this world
to lose
the game

I have scars on my body
and scars on my face
but the ones that hurt the most
were left without a trace
I have cuts from my family
and cuts from my friends
but the ones that cut the deepest
will truly never mend

Internal Stitches

I was the one
bringing you water
for your dying roots

Mother

mother sure does sleep a lot
that's all she ever wants to do
perhaps one day she will settle down
and make **A Home for Two**

mother must be lonely again
it seems there is always someone new
tomorrow she will say there is someone else
then trade him off like **Worn Out Shoes**

....and I hated every strange man I heard you sleeping with!!!!

An Angel's Touch

For the most part,
you were never there
so, I don't owe you much
the only thing I feel I missed
was a mother's loving touch

Letter from Father

'One day you'll understand this'

Don't worry about me
because I don't worry about you
I have enough on my chest
than to be worried about two

....but I never did grow to understand!

Verbal Abuse

You might think
I'm a cannibal
the way I swallow down
those words you said
and the way your **mad face**
is always in my head

Your mouth is a pit of razors that cut me with every word

The Way You Talk to Me

*....I truly believe you thought you were helping;
you just never knew how to express your love.*

Rule of Thumb

You scream at me out of love
but I cry,
because your words are hurtful and numb
so, **love me like you hate me**
my only rule of thumb

The Talk

Sometimes they're going to make you hurt
Sometimes they're going to make you bleed
Sometimes they're going to make you want
Sometimes they're going to make you need
But you can never live without them
Starvation is the reason we feed

.... We were so starved for your attention
We found it elsewhere....

It's hard to make a shadow
when nobody really cares
perhaps the image they're seeing
is not even there

Invisible Shadow

The Face in the Mirror

You don't have to tell me
that I'm **nothing**
because I know it
You don't have to tell me
that I'm **stupid**
because I think it
you don't have to tell me
that I'm **ugly**
because I see it
and the face in the mirror is **laughing**
and I can hear it

It Only Hurts When You See It

You look at me
like I'm invisible
so, you can't tell
that I'm so miserable

I feel unsure
the way you look right through
if you even care
or if I'm transparent to you

My heart is torn
and seems unfixable
like pain is not real
when you're invisible

I ask YOU everyday
if YOU still care
and YOU always
answer the same....

Until the day **I** took the mirror down

You

*.... I learned early in life
that nobody cared;
so, neither did I!*

I try and tell myself
there's nothing wrong
with walking alone
through society

'NORMAL'

is just a word
that's never fit
my anxiety

I was born an orange
in this apple orchard called life
so, I was mangled, crushed
and turned into mush
long ago by strife's ugly knife

Different

Sitting with My Hands on My Face

Don't beat me while I'm thinking
because I feel it may hurt too much
Don't rape me while I'm sleeping
because I feel you may take too much
Don't bury me while I'm breathing
because I feel it may help too much
Just help me bury the rape that's beating my thinking
this I feel I may like too much

Chapter 2

BROKEN

I want to be more than
Anything
I want to be more than
Someone
I want to be more than
Everything
I want to be the
Only one

True Love

The Song Never Sang

Love is the word I keep in my head
Love is the word that dies when I'm dead
Love is the lyric that rolls off my tongue
like a song I once knew but never got sung

Why do I waste time gluing
petals to dead flowers?

When their scent has long been faded

Old Love Letters

Unfinished Poems

I'm there waiting for you
just the way you left me
and I know you still think about me,
the way I think about you

To you it was only a moment
I think about everyday

Time of My Life

Broken Pieces

I throw your picture
against the wall everyday
wishing I could see
your pretty face bleed

But it never does

Only my fingers
and heart feel that way
from picking up
the broken pieces

Precious like a kitten
deadly as a snake
loving you will always be
My Greatest Mistake

Happy Birthday

No matter how hard
I squeezed her,
God would not
bring her back to me
No matter how loud
I screamed at him,
she still died
at only three

.... this tore the stitches from the 'already' open wounds.

Broken

You were the pieces
I was the parts
together we could not fix
our broken hearts

the dreams
we had
were crushed
long before
the lives
we lived
went running
out the door

Done Before We Started

Handprints

When the wash is done
and the stains are set
These are your handprints
still dripping wet

It's the start of a new year
and tomorrow's another day
But the pain that you've caused
will never fully go away

When you lay down to sleep
may you see nothing but their face
and feel all the emotions
that caused their disgrace

When the wash is done
and the stains are set
These are your handprints
still dripping wet

....*one day they will see....*

Return to Sender

I'm the end of a rope
You're the start of a river
They were the envelopes
we failed to deliver

Prosthetics

She pulled off my wings
and left me to die
Refusing to quit
I began to get by
Making prosthetics
I learned how to fly
And it wasn't that long
before I was back in the sky
I wish that I could say
the same for her as I
But she never could rebound
just lay around and cry
I gave her prosthetics
hoping she would try
But without any wings
she lay down and died

.... watching you suffer was never what I had hoped for;
but you chose the road you longed for....

Back Stabber

I still butter
my bread
with the same knife
you stuck
in my back

.... life moved on and so did I....

If you were an animal
I would have killed you long ago
But since you're not;
it's going to be nice and slow
Believe me;
this is not the way I wanted things to go
I tried to make things right
Just So You Know

she was always swallowing razor blades
I was just there to clean up the mess she made

Scapegoat

....and I covered up all your lies;
until they could no longer be hid!

Lock of Hair

The day I can no longer fly,
I'll run
The day I can no longer run,
I'll walk
The day I can no longer walk,
I'll crawl
The day I can no longer crawl,
I'll pretend
and dream of days when I held you,
until I can hold you once again

She Loves Me Not

If by my own choice
I'd have been a flower
Possibly a rose
or maybe a sun
But most likely
I'd have been the one
that ended with,
she loves me not
Only to be thrown to the ground
stomped and left to rot
The hated one
that's always forgot
she loves me,
she loves me not

A Blind Eye

I remember
how the pain
hurts you
more than me
But with my
eyes closed
it's never
clear to see

No one lies as much as you
When you open your mouth,
I know it's not true

Pathological

Burning Desire

I'm pushing myself away from the fire
You can no longer hold me as your own
I'll no longer be your burning desire
My heart's been turned to stone
You have stripped me of skin
and left me as bone
But I'll still walk away from the fire
and leave you burning all alone

....and it still burns you today
knowing I finally got away!

Stitched together
Pieces of my heart
Left forever
This world you tore apart

Our Old House

....it was never the fault of our children; yet they suffer!

My heart was a door
that had been opened and closed
so many times
I finally nailed it shut

Do Not Enter

You said you could never love anyone else
and without me you would rather die
But there you are still breathing
and loving another guy

Dead in Love

Watching from outside a window
at the life I once had
My wife with her new husband
and my kids with a new dad

The Life I Once Had

In my hands
I hold your life
When my pen
becomes a knife
I can write you out
like I wrote you in
When my knife
becomes a pen

Dead in My Head

The prettiest eyes
I ever did see
belonged
to a girl
who couldn't
see me

Blind

.... *you had the world and gave it away!*

New Hair Color

Wiping the stains from my hands
was like erasing her from my life
Changing my hair color
had nothing to do
with the disappearance of my ex-wife

If I Could Hurt You with What I Say

I'll tell you I'm a writer
so, I don't scare you with what I say
If I were just a normal person
you could have me locked away
But since I'm a poet
that makes everything seem okay
so, I can share with you all my obsessions
and you'll think it's just for play
I'll remind you that I'm a writer
and I can't hurt you with what I say

I wish I could be
at your funeral
and be the last
to close the door
But I'll be
too busy
celebrating,
knowing I won't
have to take
your shit
anymore

Last to Close the Door

Chapter 3

I Hate the World Because the World Hates me

Smile

Once I get dirty
I can never get clean
to wipe off my
hands
of all that I've seen
For *life is not pretty*
when living a lie
and the *smile* on your face
says waiting to die

Burn After Reading

In God's eyes
I'm a murderer
for I've killed 1000's in my head
In God's eyes
I'm a rapist
for I've wanted 1000's in my bed
In God's eyes
I'm a sadist
for I'd rather feel pain than dread
In God's eyes
I'm a monster
for I'm walking through this life dead

...and the World Would Not Care

No smile upon my face
No sunlight left in space
No flowers in my cup
all living drying up
No happy songs to sing
No winter turning spring
No such thing as good luck
in a world that doesn't give a fuck

World War M3

How can I keep living,
in a world that wants me dead
And how can I keep fighting,
when I struggle to get out of bed
Medications aren't helping,
the constant war inside my head
And I can't stand to be around people,
whose conversations are a thing of dread
I have nothing left to comfort me,
but the cuts that I drain red
And my body is scarred like a battle field,
from previous cuts I've bled
So how can I keep fighting,
this war inside my head
And how long can I keep living,
in a world where I'm already dead

I apologize for being stupid,
and for things I do so wrong
I apologize for being different,
and trying to fit where I don't belong
I apologize for breathing,
in a world that wants me drowned
I apologize for living,
when nobody wants me around

Fitting Circles into Squares

It feels like the first time I've spoken
My mind goes blank
and I'm left fumbling my fingers,
searching for thoughts that won't come out
I would like to speak to you,
but the words seem hopeless
So, I say nothing at all

How I Speak to Strangers

Had I any use for air
I would breathe
But I haven't done that,
since the day you walked out on me

Life

For Halloween I want to be Me

I used to wear a mask for Halloween
Now Halloween wears a mask for me
I used to pretend I was a monster
Now the monsters pretend to be me

I always thought,
you were my friend
We laughed
We talked
You were always around

It wasn't until the day,
I took that mirror down
I realized
I was alone

My Own Reflection

Bird in a Cage

They think I like singing
but how could they be so wrong
Mistaking my screams
for a beautiful song

They watch me through windows
like a bird in a cage
By taming they're helping
remove all my rage

I flounder about
bouncing off walls
Crying for anyone
to hear my calls

I just stare out the windows
waiting to die
And watch as other birds
still fly in the sky

Put on a Happy Face

It's the first impression you see
It's a cover up - a lie
It's not really me
It's to bring you comfort
Because no one wants to be friends,
with someone who lives their life in denial
But put on a happy face
and they can accept a person,
Who would wear a fake smile

I must look like a work of art
the way I paint this smile on daily

Frown

*.... it's hard for people to realize,
it's the ones who smile the biggest
that are suffering the most*

Mask

Behind the mask,
you cannot see
This smile I wear,
is not meant for me
It hides the truth,
to which I lie
Behind the mask,
I wait to die

No one can save me
from me,
but me
The man in the mirror's
reflection,
can't see
He is too beautiful
to be,
ugly
So, I smash
all the mirrors,
to be set free

Ugly

Although my skin hides
the skeleton inside of me
It fails to cover
the monster I see
For only I know all
his lies and distrust
Which leads me to hate
his face with disgust

Disgusting

Metamorphous

How can I be someone else,
if I no longer care to be myself
I'll wrap myself in tomorrow,
until I metamorphose
into something else
And fly away...
Like I was never anything at all

It's hard to stay positive
in a world with so much hate
When everyone you know
is trying to manipulate
And they would rather see you fail
than help you to succeed
or show a little support
when a friend is all you need

Friends

Butterfly Wings

I
pulled
the wings
off a butterfly
just to watch it die
Because it's beautiful to see
something else sharing this pain of life
with me
I place its wings under my pillow
to help me sleep at night
and dream of better days
when this butterfly
still had
flight

FADe

I don't want to think
    when I'm alone
I don't want to cry
    help to you
I don't want to feel
    with empty emotions
But there is nothing more
    therapy can do
I don't want to look
    in the mirror
I don't want to face
    another day
I don't want anymore
    prescriptions
I just want the world
    to fade away

Rid Me Dead

Facing the demons
Inside my head
To rid of them
I must be dead
Alone in dark
I fear their call
But I'm alone
With padded wall
I cannot grasp
what is not real
For how I see
is how I feel
I can't escape
From my own head
I beg the lord
come rid me dead

I was
choked
by all
humanity's
ignorance
and nearly
aspirated
on my own
anxiety

Humanity

Self-destruct
or self-implode
always a martyr
who carries the load

Martyr

If This is What You Want to Hear

The world is perfect
and everything is right
If you are *Not Straight*
Christian
or White
The world is perfect
and everything is okay
If you are a *Muslim*
Atheist
or Gay
The world is perfect
And everything is free
If you are *Not Healthy*
Honest
or Supporting History
The world is perfect
if this is what you want to hear
If you are *Not Working*
on Welfare
or a Criminal
You have nothing else to fear

Old Country Song

Nobody cares
how anyone is feeling
Everyone is narcissistic
and everybody is killing
Nothing seems right
unless something is going wrong
As we live unhappy lives
like an old country song

Life's Little Whores

On our knees we pray
begging for another day
Just to live a life
were forced to work away

Here's some good advice

'Never try to save'
Money makes us whores to life
we can't take to our grave

A recipe for the mentally well

- 1 parts sadness
- 2 pieces sympathy
- 1 chunk of anger
- "Mix together with apathy"

- Stir in a batch of confusion
- Adding 2 pinches of old age
- 2 pieces of anguish
- 1 heaping scoop of rage

- Stir depression until anxiety is fully changed
- Bake until bipolar disoprder no longer seems deranged

- Allow to cool
- Enjoy your Varyla pills

Feeble

There's always a hurtful storm
raging wars throughout my brain
It's a quiet soothing voice
like a slow falling rain
His face is in the mirror laughing
because he knows that I'm not strong
So, I break his feeble image
that's been staring back so long
I'll take his broken pieces
and cut deep into my past
Then watch the memories fade away
until I'm freed at last

Forgotten by Time

A shell of myself
or who I once claimed to be
Finding out now
I am not what you see
The more you keep searching
the more pieces don't rhyme
Missing or broken
Forgotten by time

Never Trust the Man in the Moon

To live in the day
looks to be so much fun
Vicariously living
through the eyes of the sun
Stalking the world
like a creature of the night
Hiding from tomorrow
like a vampire from the light

I Want to Be Solomon Grundy

I just want to lay in bed
all day long
Cover up my head
and listen to sad songs
I want to feel sorry for myself
and feed my apathetic need
I want to uncover my scars
and pick until they bleed
I want to wallow in the pain
like my existence is a crime
I want to end up like Solomon Grundy
from my favorite child hood nursery rhyme

You can change the way you see with your eyes
But you can't erase the mistake once the ink dries

Sometimes They Follow You Home

Work of Art

Sometimes I'd like to kill myself
But don't understand why?
If I could make the name
'Suicide'
sound beautiful
I'd really like to try
Perhaps they would put me in a frame
and call me a work of art
As the vultures smile and take pictures
of a suicide's broken heart

Silence

I cry out
for help
But
nobody's
there
Where are
the people
pretending
to care

Gently

until my heart
stops feeling
or I fail to exist
gently
drag the razor
across my wrist

As the clock slowly ticks life away
Death gets closer with every passing day

Vacation from Life

It's getting easier for me to find reasons to do it;
Than not

Eat a Bullet

I left it on the foot of the bed
-the last note I wrote you
Just before I walked to the shed
I left it there, so it would be read
-the last note I wrote you
Just before I put a gun to my head
I left it, so it would haunt you once I dead
-the last note I wrote you
With only a short message that said,

I'm sorry
Sincerely yours,
Alfred Gremsly

Another Failed Attempt

I'm at the edge of my rope
and the end of a gun
May this be the last day
I end what's begun
I'm standing on a ledge
with nowhere to run
May this be the last time
I see the sun
I'm at the bottom of a bottle
of the pills I can't resist
I'm on the edge of a blade
Sliding across my wrist
I'm at the end of the world
waiting for someone to hear my call
If no one is there to answer
I was meant to take the fall
But on the other end
a voice is pleading for my life
As I spit out the pills
and throw down the knife
I back away from the ledge
and lay down the gun

I thank my new angel
who has just led me to the sun
I think of all that's good
and the reasons to exist
I tattoo their lifeline number
proudly across my wrist
I learned that life is beautiful
but none of us are exempt
And gained a new respect for love
with another failed attempt

"National Suicide Prevention Lifeline"

1-800-273-8255

HELP

Chapter 4

Upside Down
Frown

What starts as a poem to heal you
May end up the book that saves you

Keep Reading

No More Rain

These eyes have seen hurt
These eyes have seen pain
These eyes have cried tears
that feel like rain
These eyes have seen hate
These eyes have seen rage
These eyes have been treated
like a dog in a cage
These eyes have seen anger
These eyes are now sane
These eyes will not cry
another drop of rain

Scream

The air is free
so why don't we scream
Let go of the anger
That's holding our dream
Pour out the emotions
that keep us enraged
By not letting go
we live life encaged

The air is free
so why don't we scream
Pour out the emotions
and live out our dreams

Miracle

How can you love what you do not know?
How can the sun make seedlings grow?
How can you believe in what isn't there?

In a world with no GOD I see him everywhere!

It tells you what to do
It tells you what to say
It tells you how to live
It tells you how to pray

The Bible

Confess

You won't start to breathe
Until you get the demons off your chest

Paper Cuts

Never
leave
the stitches
in for so long
you begin
to like
the feeling
of being
hurt

Half Empty

if you're
waiting
for a
positive
answer
from a
negative
person
the outcome
is always
the same
and the
cup is
always
half empty

Cover to Cover

No matter how bad the chapters get,
finish the one you're in
before moving on
to another
book

No one can save me
from me,
but me
The man in the mirror's
reflection,
can't see
He is too beautiful
to be
ugly
So, I smash
all the mirror's,
to be
set free

Ugly

Fear of God

I smile instead of frowning
I laugh instead of cry
I joke instead of complaining
I live instead of die
I give instead of taking
I love instead of hate
I feel instead of bleeding,
from fear of what awaits

Hanging on to all you know
From the worn-out rope
and can't let go

Letting Go of the Past

A Lesson Learned

How do you forget
what you can still remember
When you can taste the rage
and feel the anger
How does the nail
forgive the hammer
While licking wounds
from a lesson learned

Death Bed

Don't start to cry
before I die
There is a reason
And I'll tell you why
I'm going home
Where angels fly
Where streets are gold
And ground is sky
Don't start to cry
Before I die
Just hold my hand
And say good bye
One final chance
Before I fly
I'm going home
So say good bye

Can you imagine
Becoming of something out of me?
Can you imagine
Making my dreams a reality?
Can you imagine
Becoming of something you wanted to be?
Can you imagine
'Me' pulling myself from the misery?

When everything is ugly it makes everything seem more beautiful

Pretty Ugly

Dying to Be Free

It took killing myself
to find new life
and the person
I had wanted to be
And letting go
of my once dead past
was the only way
that I could be free

Words I Say in the Mirror

Winner
~~Loser~~ Achiever
Nice
Caring
~~SAD~~ happy
~~Different~~ Normal
~~Stupid~~ Smart
Dependable
~~Sad~~ Happy
Truthful
Encouraging
~~Hateful~~ Loving
~~Ugly~~ Beautiful
Thoughtful
Strong
Believer
Brilliant
~~Sad~~ HAPPY
Leader
'HAPPY'
Joyful
Father
Friend
"BLESSED"

New Born

I thought God
had buried me
in the
darkness
But in
truth
he had
planted me
with hopes
that I
would
grow
in the light

To Hate Is to Love

To hate
what used
to be,
means
you must
have once
loved
what is
no more!
So,
I'll spend
the rest
of my
life
not
hating
you

Book on a Shelf

Be happy with the love you have for yourself
Be happy with those around you
and be willing to put
the past on a
shelf
Be
happy
that you lived it
but never have to again
Be happy that it's over and a new one
has just began

The Day I Met *You*

Until the day I found *you*
I thought love
was supposed to hurt
Then *you* pulled me
from the pain
and washed away
the dirt

You taught me that love
was the reason I should
You taught me to live
and believe that I could
When no one else did
You told me I would
When life was so bad
You made everything good

Until the day I found *you*
I thought love
was supposed to hurt
Then *you* pulled me
from the pain
and washed away
the dirt

Two Angels

God gave me two angels,
to survive the human race
A daughter named *Jillien*,
Another *Nolie Grace*
In my times of doubt,
I need only look at their face
and it's enough to remind me,
there's a heaven above this place

100 Candles

On my 20th year of life
I placed 40 candles on my cake
20 for the first bad years
and 20 for every year a mistake

On my 40th year of life
I placed 80 candles on my cake
20 for both my children
and 40 more, for years to make

On my 80th year of life
I'll place 100 candles on my cake
80 for every God given year
and 20 more, for years to slowly take

Author's Note

This book seems like so long ago!
It's a story that dwelled inside my head and begged to be let out.
I never fully grasped the control I allowed it to have on my life.
Until the day I set down and began to write. And slowly the
demons that held me down for so long, started releasing little
pieces of my broken soul.
And I remember the feeling as it started coming over me!
It was something I had not felt in a lifetime!
Like a thousand knives stabbing my chest! 'Could this be love'?
But after finishing chapters 1-3, I realized I had let go of the pain
and hurt that had controlled my life.
I was free from the memories of a saddened childhood.
The hatred toward a mother who had put men before her kids.
The anger toward a father who had used his voice and words as
a weapon and means of punishment. A man who had abandoned
us in our time of need.
The bitter hatred toward an ex-wife who had committed adul-
tery and taken everything I had worked so hard for. The mother
of my children who had given away everything for her addiction
to drugs! Not even the love of her own children could pull her
back from despair.
The anger toward God, who I blamed for my broken childhood;
for the death of my unborn child and the reason my life had been
so hard.
I forgave!
I felt warmth!
I felt love!
I finally healed!
Most importantly; I felt alive!
And I smiled!

Alfred Gremsly

CPSIA information can be obtained
at www.ICGtesting.com
Printed in the USA
BVHW031839251119
564781BV00001B/104/P